BUILDING A HOUSE
A Step-by-Step Guide

By
Nat Council

TURNER PUBLISHING COMPANY
PADUCAH, KENTUCKY

Turner Publishing Company

Copyright © 1995 Nat Council
Publishing Rights:
Turner Publishing Company
Robert J. Martin, Chief Editor

Library of Congress Catalog No.
95-061237
ISBN: 978-1-56311-218-8

CONTENTS

Introduction:

Building a house may be one of the most important things a person will ever do in their lifetime. Many people feel that building a house is a very trying experience. I believe, however, that building a house should be challenging, and enjoyable.

I have been in the construction industry for more than 20 years. I chose the residential field because of the challenge and enjoyment this field offers. I have built houses from small to large, lower priced to very high priced and have learned that everyone involved can enjoy the process if they choose wisely.

The information included in this book will help to make the process of building a house a more enjoyable and fulfilling experience.

I hope that you will use this information to make your experience just that.

Yours Truly,

Nat Council
Council Construction, Inc.

Step #1:   Financial arrangements

One of the biggest mistakes that many people make when planning to build a house is building more than they can afford. It is impossible to make this an enjoyable experience when you have doubts about your ability to pay for what you are building. It is very important that you know what you can afford, and build within your means.

The following is a list of suggestions to assist you in making your financial arrangements:

Set-up a meeting with a loan officer at your local bank or other lending facility and discuss the following:
1) Your current financial situation
2) The amount of money you can afford to spend
3) The various types of loans that are available
4) The interest rates, length of time for pay-off, monthly payment
5) The possibility of government backed loans available: VA, FHA
6) Down payments, closing costs, recording fees
7) Using property as a source of security for your financing
8) The appraisal process involved in determining value for your house
9) The location, and the effect it will have on the appraisal value

The above suggestions are points that you should be aware of when trying to determine the amount of money that you can afford to spend to build your house. You should remember that lending facilities are in business to loan money. It is a good policy to visit more than one lending facility to make sure that you can secure the best possible financial arrangements that are available to you. You may find that you can save a great deal of money by simply checking the various financing that is available. You should be very sure that you are comfortable with the amount of money that you can spend on your house. You should not put yourself in a strained financial situation, or the fun and excitement of building your house will not be there for you.

NOTES:

Step #2:   Choosing a house plan

After you have determined the amount of money you can invest in building your house, you can now decide on what to build. You should begin by checking the prices of newer houses that are for sale in your area. This will give you an idea of what type and size house you can build in your price range. You should remember, however, that the total cost includes both the house and the lot on which it is built.

After looking at the various types and sizes of houses that are in your price range, it is time to get the plans for your house. There are several ways to get house plans. It is preferable to have a set of plans drawn by an architect. You can then be part of the decision making process regarding the style, size, room sizes lay-out interior and exterior features. The architect can design your house specifically for you and your situation.

The most common way to pick a house plan, however, is from books and magazines available at your local bookstore. You should look at as many of these books as possible to see what is available. Remember to look at houses that are similiar in size and style to those that you have already seen for sale to keep you in your approximate price range. It is best to pick two or three house plans that appeal to you, then begin to look closely at the one that offers you the most of what you like. I recommend that you then choose a plan, order it, and begin to look at it. The costs of these plans vary with each book, but most are very reasonable in cost in comparison to the cost of using an architect. You should remember that you cannot get an accurate price on what you want to build without a set of plans from which to work.

A set of plans is necessary if you want to build efficiently and effectively. Everyone involved in the process of building your house needs a guide from which to work and your plans act as that guide. You may want to make some changes in your plans to meet your particular situation, but the plans are still the basic guide from which everyone works to build your house.

After choosing a plan that you want to use, you are now ready to choose a site on which to build your house. In the following step, we will discuss the information you need to consider when choosing your location.

NOTES:

Step #3   Choosing a location

A very important factor to consider when choosing a location, is the impact on the value of your house. The appraisal value of your house depends upon where the house is located. Most lending institutions will have an appraisal made to determine what the value of the house will be in order to determine the loan value. In most situations, your house should be built in an area where the houses are similiar in size and price range. If you choose to locate your house in an area where the houses are not, you should consult with the person who is making your financial arrangements. This may cause you to reconsider where you want to build.

The following is a list of items you should consider when choosing your location:

1) Sizes and styles of houses in the area
2) Value of property in the are
3) Property taxes
4) Restrictions and set back
5) School districts
6) Price of the property
7) Cost of clearing and prepartion
8) Cost of installing driveway for accessability
9) Availability of utilities
   Water
   Sewer
   Gas
   Electricity
   Telephone
   Cable Television
10) Cost of tap-on fees for utilities
11) Installation costs of utilities, if not available

Before you decide to purchase the property, you need specific information about the property. I recommend that you following procedure in order to gain the necessary information.

The best way to determine the value of the houses and property is to contact a local real estate agent or appraiser. The cost for their services will be well worth what you spend to have the assurance that what you are paying for the property is in line with the value.

Discuss the availablity of utilities with the person selling the property If the utilities are available, are the tap on fees included in the purchase price. If the fees are not included in the purchase price of the property, you should be informed as to their amounts. If the person selling the property does not know about the utilities, you should then contact a representative from each of your local utility companies to discuss the availability of the utilities, cost of installation to your location, tap-on fees,and time of installation. This may have a great deal of impact on the price and value of the property that you are considering.

The next factors to consider about your location are clearing and preparation costs and the cost to install your driveway for accessability. These factors should be included in the cost of construction of your house. The situation that you are faced with, however, is deciding on whether to purchase the property before you have received prices from builders. The best way to determine an approximate cost for these items is to contact one or more of the builders you are considering. You should then ask them to meet with you to look over the property and get their input about the conditions. After meeting with the builder, or builders, ask them to give you an approximate cost of clearing, lot preparation, and installation of the drive. You should be aware that this will only be an approximate cost, but it will give you a general idea of what the total cost of your land investment will be.

After looking into the various aspects of the location you are considering, you will then be able to decide what the cost, value, and total investment of the propery will be. These factors will assist you in determining the best location for your house.

A good location is very important and you should be very deliberate in your search to find the property best suited for your situation.

After you have decided upon the location for your house, you are now ready to choose the builder that will work with you in building your house. We will go over some things that you need to consider, when deciding upon your builder, in the next step of your guide.

NOTES:

Step #4 Choosing a builder

Choosing a builder is the most important aspect of building a house. As you continue to read the information that is provided for you in this guide, you will see that your builder is the most important person to you in the process of building your house.

The factors that you should consider when choosing your builder are: their qualifications, communication ablility, reputation, quality of construction, and finally, pricing.

There are two very simple ways to get information about the various builders in your area. First, talk to people who have built a house. Second, talk to representatives or sales persons at your local lumber companies. You should use both of these sources to get information about the builders you are considering. The following are topics you should discuss with your prospective builders:

1) Types, styles, sizes, and price ranges of houses completed
2) Quality of materials used
3) Quality of the sub-contractors used
4) References from previous customers
5) Communication skills with customers, suppliers, and sub-contractors
6) Payment of bills and general business ability
7) Pricing ability and accuracy for the houses

You should remember that you need to feel comfortable with the builder you choose. You should use the builder with whom you have confidence and trust. This will make the building process easier and more enjoyable.

Many people choose a builder based upon price only, and that is a big mistake. You should remember the saying: "you get what you pay for" and that is certainly true. A good builder will not always give you the cheapest price, but in most cases, will give you the best price available for the kind of house that you should want to build.

In the steps to follow, I will give you information on what to discuss with builders concerning the pricing structure of your house. This will give you some guidelines with which to work in order to assure that you are getting the same pricing structure from each of the builders that you talk to. The next step in our guide will give you information concerning the topics that you should discuss with the builders who are pricing your house. This same information will also help you during the process of building your house.

NOTES:

Step # 5   Go over the job with the builder

These are the topics that you should discuss with the prospective builder. You want to be sure that each builder's bid is figured using the same factors.

1) Go over the plans to discuss any changes or modifications you wish to make
2) Check on the necessary permits, fees, and insurance that is needed
3) The cost of clearing and preparing the property
4) Cost of the driveway to allow accessibility to the site
5) Utilities for the site: water, power, sewer, phone, cable
6) Type of foundation needed for your house
7) Building materials used for the framing of the house

8) Windows and exterior doors
9) Type of exterior finishes that you want to use for your house
10) Discuss fireplaces, if applicable, and the type that is best suited for your house
11) Electrical costs including the light fixture allowance
12) Plumbing: including the plumbing fixture allowance
13) Heating and air conditioning
14) Sheet metal work and flashings that will be needed
15) Insulation
16) Interior walls and ceilings: materials and finishes
17) Interior trimwork
18) Cabinetry allowance
19) Hardware and accessory allowance
20) Floor covering allowance
21) Exterior surfaces allowance
22) Landscaping allowance

In the steps to follow, I will give you information about each of the topics listed above. You should remember, however, that your builder is the person who needs to build your house. The information that I am providing is simply to give you a general working knowledge of what needs to be done. This will help you to feel more comfortable with the situation since you have a general idea of the steps involved with the building of your house.

After you have met with various builders, reviewed their qualifications, reviewed the pricing estimates, and thought about the situation completely, it is now time for you to choose your builder.

NOTES:

Step # 6 Planning the actual start of building your house

There are some things that you should keep in mind during the building project. The most important of which is to talk to your builder. You should never, never assume anything. Your builder should be your advisor during the entire time the house is being built. You should ask your builder any questions that you may have at any time during the project.

The following is a list of topics that need to be covered before the actual process of building begins. Plan a meeting with your builder to discuss these topics:

1) The plans and the job site
2) Builder's risk insurance (homeowner's responsibility)
3) Homeowner's insurance
4) Builder's insurance: Workers' Compensation, Liability
5) Builder's starting date and working schedule
6) Utilities on the jobsite—water, power, sewer, gas, phone, cable
7) Preparation of the site—clearing, driveway, location of house on site
8) Permits and fees that need to be secured before beginning
9) Time frame— There are many decisions that must be made throughout the building process. Many of these decisions must be made well in advance.

Step # 7 Preparing the site

The next step in the building process is to prepare the site. The following is a list of things to be considered when preparing your site:

1) Consider any trees or other natural items you want to try to save
2) Locate your house in the most suited place for looks and efficiency
3) Restrictions and set back lines
4) The correct route of the driveway or driveways
5) Consider distances of drives, utilities, and visibility when locating the house
6) Consider drainage when locating the house on the site
7) The site should be clear of debris
8) Install the driveway or driveways while the heavy equipment is on the site
9) Install the water and temporary power on the site for use during constrution
10) After clearing is completed, locate the house on the site and prepare for the foundation

Step # 8   Foundation

Before pouring the foundation, the builder will discuss the conditions of the site with you. If your builder feels that there are any problems with the condition of the soil or other problems, these should be addressed before starting to dig. It is very, very important for you to remember that your house is only as good as the foundation on which it is built. The following is a discussion of the various types of foundations:

Foundation with a crawl space under living area:

This type of foundation is perhaps the most widely used because of the under the house accessability for the installation of the various mechanical items needed during the construction process.

The crawl space installation process is as follows:

1) Dig and pour a footing: depth, width, size and reinforcement as per codes
2) Lay concrete blocks on which to set the framing of the house, as per codes
3) Install proper fill, grading and drainage piping under house after blockwork
4) Provide positive drainage to assure that water cannot be trapped under the house
5) Provide vertical reinforcement and pour concrete in block cells, as per codes
6) Provide anchor bolts poured in block cells to secure framing, as per codes
7) Provide termite treatment and vapor barrier over fill under the house

Basement with living area above:

This type of foundation is popular on a site that has a natural grade that will allow the installation of a basement without a major expense to the owner of the house. There are two ways that a basement can be installed:

1) Poured concrete walls with steel reinforcement and concrete blocks with vertical and horizontal reinforcement. We will go over both types of installation, but the poured concrete wall system is by far the better installation.

2) Poured Concrete Walls:

Lay-out and dig out the area to grade
Dig and pour a footing with reinforcement steel as per codes
Forming of the wall system with reinforcement, vertical and horizontal, per codes
Poured concrete inside the form system with high-strength concrete, as per codes
Removal of the forms and cleaning the walls and footings to prep for waterproofing
Provide suitable waterproofing material on the outside of poured walls and footing
Install drainage piping around perimeter of the walls to provide for relief drainage
Install filterable gravel around perimeter of the walls over the drainage piping
Install filterable gravel on inside of walls on which to pour the concrete floor
Provide termite treatment, vapor barrier, and reinforcement wire over fill
Pour concrete floor over fill with high-strength concrete
Anchor bolts should be installed in the wall and floor pours to anchor framing

Concrete block walls:

Steps for this process are the same except for the walls and waterproofing. The reinforcement is with vertical steel and dura-wall block reinforcement for the horizontal. The waterproofing system should be much more complex than with the poured wall system because of the potential of cracking in the block walls that will allow water to penetrate the surfaces. I recommend a rubber type waterproofing system of some kind that will prevent this water from penetrating the surfaces of the blocks to the inside of the basement. You should discuss all aspects of basement installation with your builder before making your final decision on what type installation you will use.

The next type of foundation that is used in house construction is concrete floor and footing in lieu of crawl space type construction. There are two ways to install the concrete floor system.

The first is to incorporate the footing and the floor in one pour. This process is used quite often in climates where the ground is not subjected to freeze and thaw conditions.

The process is as follows:
1) Prep the building site to the closest grade possible
2) Set perimeter forms as to the lay-out of the house
3) Inside the forms, dig a footing area to widen and thicken the edges along the forms
4) Install the mechanical rough-ins as to the lay-out of the house (check carefully)
5) Install filterable gravel over entire area and grade
6) Provided termite treatment, vapor barrier, and reinforcement wire over fill
7) Pour concrete floor and widened footing area with high-strength concrete
8) Anchor bolts should be placed in concrete as the pour is made to anchor framing

The alternate process of this type foundation should be used in areas where the footing needs to be installed below the frost line of the area. This factor should be discussedwith your builder before any type foundation is installed, especially with this type. The process of this type of foundation is:
1) Dig and pour footing with reinforcement as per local building codes
2) Use forming blocks or forms on footing for perimeter lay-out of the house
3) Install fill inside the forming system to rough grade
   Complete the process by following the steps listed in the above section.

After the foundation is completed, you are now ready to move to the process of building the structure of the house.

NOTES:

The quality of the materials used to frame your house are very important. The following are questions that you should ask your builder:

1) Will the material have a certified grade stamp from the supplier?
2) Will the floor framing members be 2"x 10" or 2"x 12" material?
3) How will the framing members be placed? 16"—19 1/4"—or 24" centers?
4) What type of sub-flooring system will be used? 1 layer or 2 layers?
5) Will the walls be framed with 2"x 4" studs or 2"x 6" studs?
6) Will the ceiling joist and rafters be 2"x 6" or 2"x 8" material?
7) What type of roof decking will be used?
8) What type of bracing system will be used for walls, joists, and roof?
9) What type of special fasteners or ties are needed for framing in your area?
10) What type of exterior sheathing will be used?
11) What type of roofing material will be used?
12) What type of windows and exterior doors will be used?

The items listed above should be discussed with your builder. Each builder has a system by which they work. This system uses the materials and labor that is best suited for your builder. You should discuss the system with your builder using the above listed questions as your guide to help you feel comfortable with that system.

NOTES:

Step # 10   Framing the house

The following is a list of topics to consider before your builder starts to frame the house.

Discuss the following exterior details with your builder:
1) Exterior lay-out
2) Location of windows and doors
3) Roof: pitch (slope)—overhang—ventilation
4) Roof structures: dormers—decorative vents—accent trims
5) Wall and roof flashings and sheet metal work

Discuss the following interior details:
1) Room locations and sizes
2) Closet locations and sizes
3) Door locations, swings, and sizes
4) Stairway location and lay-out

Discuss the following framing details:
1) Cathedral ceilings
2) Vaulted ceilings
3) Tray ceilings
4) Arches
5) Nitches
6) Soffit framing

Discuss attic accessability and storage potential.

It is important for you to remember that changes cost money. You should be sure to go over any part of the framing process with your builder before the work is done. You should discuss anything that you feel is important to you about the lay-out of the house, interior or exterior before the work is done, or you may cost yourself a great deal of time and money. Your builder will assist you in this process. You should keep in your mind that your builder has been through this process before; therefore, you should ask questions about any part of the framing process that is not clear to you.

NOTES:

Step # 11   Exterior wall finish and trim

After the framing process is completed, it is time for the exterior wall finish and trim process. You should choose the material that is best suited for your particular house. The important factor to consider when choosing exterior finishes is maintenance and upkeep. Most people want to minimize maintenance; therefore, consider this factor when choosing your exterior finishes. The easiest way to choose the type of exterior finish you like is to drive around your city and pick a house with the finish scheme that appeals to you.

Exterior trim consists of roof overhang, porches, accent trim and railings. The following materials are used for exterior trimwork:

     Exterior graded wood that must be painted or stained
     Exterior graded wood that can be left unfinished
     Pressure treated material that can be stained or left unfinished
     Ornamental ironwork that must be painted
     Aluminum and vinyl cladding over framed members
     Aluminum guttering that is pre-finished
     Plastic or fiberglass materials that can be pre-finished or painted
     Concrete or masonry materials

You should discuss the exterior trimwork of your house with your builder to decide which materials and finishes are best for your house.

Exterior wall finish surfaces are also included when considering the maintenance and up-keep of your house. The following is a list of materials used for exterior finishes:

     Brick
     Stone
     Rock
     Wood siding
     Hard board siding
     Aluminum or vinyl siding
     Stucco: vinyl base or cement base

You should discuss which of these materials is best suited for your house. Your builder will explain cost, availability, and other details about these materials. You should discuss all aspects of these materials before choosing which one to use.

Now that we have discussed the framing and exterior finishes, we now are ready to discuss the process of finishing the interior of the house.

NOTES:

The most important factor to consider about the electrical work in your house, is that it must be done by a qualified person. This is a very important area and you should discuss with your builder and your electrician about the following topics:

1) Size of electrical service to be installed
2) Provisions made for any future electical needs
3) Location of service on your house
4) Wire sizes to all devices and equipment
5) Amount and location of smoke detectors
6) Location and number of receptacles in each room
7) Switched receptacles in any room
8) Location of switches in each room
9) Special switches in any area or room
10) Type and color of switches and receptacles
11) Provisions for appliances, heat/air equipment, etc.
12) Provisions for any special equipment, appliances, etc.
13) Lighting for each room:
    Location of fixtures
    Type of fixtures
    Number of fixtures
    Accent lighting for any areas
14) Ceiling fans for any areas
15) Provisions for any exterior or landscape lighting
16) Location and number of phone outlets
17) Provisions for the number of phone lines to be used
18) Location and number of cable television outlets
19) Alarm system
20) Intercom system
21) Stereo or Sound system
22) Combination systems

The above listed items are the areas to be covered with your builder and electrician before the work begins. This is another area that should be discussed very carefully in order to avoid leaving out some particular feature that you want included in the electrical work of your house. I will repeat myself in stating that changes are costly and you should discuss each part of the finishing process with your builder in great detail. This will help you to minimize or avoid costly changes or corrections that could occur.

The next step to consider is the plumbing for your house. We will discuss plumbing in the next step in this guide.

NOTES:

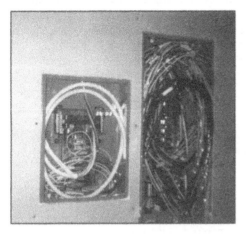

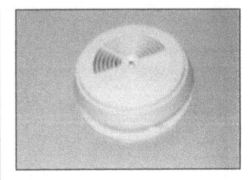

The installation of the plumbing in your house should be done by a qualified person. It also is a very important to discuss the following topics with your builder and the plumber:

1) Sewer service provided: septic system installation or tie-in to public system
2) Size of sewer line provided from house to sewage system
3) Size of water line service provided to the house
4) Gas line piping for appliances, fireplaces and equipment with cut-valves provided
5) Provisions for any special equipment: circulating pump, water softeners, etc.
6) Location of exterior hose bibs
7) Water heaters: number needed and location
8) Kitchen sink: location, type, size, and faucetry
9) Bar sink: location, type, size, and faucetry
10) Utility sink: location, type, size, and faucetry
11) Washer and dryer location
12) Garbage disposal: type and size
13) Dishwasher location
14) Refrigerator location for icemaker line installation
15) Provisions for any special appliances: ice makers, fountains, pumps
16) Bathtubs and showers: location, type, size, hand, and faucetry
17) Bathroom sinks: location, type, size, and faucetry
18) Pedistal sinks: location, type, size, and faucetry
19) Toilets: location, type, and size.

The plumbing lay-out and locations are very critical. Changes in plumbing rough-ins are extremely costly, therefore, it is important to be very systematic in the lay-out process. You should go over the plumbing lay-out on a fixture to fixture basis with your builder and plumber to avoid costly and time consuming mistakes.

Heating and air conditioning is the next step to discuss.

NOTES:

Step # 14 Heating and air conditioning

The installation of the heating and air conditioning system in your house should be done by qualified people. The important factors to consider about the people doing the work are: installation, service, and maintenance. Your heating and air conditioning equipment is only as good as it is installed, serviced and maintained. The following is a list of items to be discussed with your builder and the heat and air person:

1) Type of heating fuel to be used in your situation: natural gas, LP gas, electric
2) Type, size, and number of systems needed for your house
3) Quality and reliability of equipment, including the Energy Efficiency Rating
4) Warranty provisions and conditions
5) Service and maintenance provisions
6) Provisions for accessory equipment: air cleaners, humidifiers
7) Gas line piping for appliances, fireplaces, and equipment with cut-off valves
8) Locations of units, gas meter
9) Size and location of concrete pads for equipment
10) Type and sizes of ductwork, insulation, and registers
11) Locations of supply registers for each room
12) Locations of return air grilles
13) Locations for control devices
14) Venting for bath fans, appliances, equipment, etc.
15) Provisions for any sheet metal work or flashings.

By dicussing the above topics with your builder, you will have a good understanding of the type of system that will be installed in your house.

The next step to consider is the insulation.

NOTES:

Insulating your house has an important influence on the cost of operation of your heating and air conditioning equipment. You should discuss with your builder installing the best possible insulation available for your house. Insulation is rated in R-Value. The higher the R-Value (Resistance Value), the more insulation value is achieved. The thickness and density of the insulation material determine the R-Value.

You should discuss the insulation of the following areas with your builder:

1) Floor insulation
2) Exterior wall insulation
3) Interior wall insulation for helping with sound
4) Ceiling insulation
5) Attic insulation

Your builder will assist you in deciding about what type of insulation is best for your particular house. You should make the point very clear that you want to install the materials that will provide the most energy efficiency available for your house.

The cost that you incur for insulation will be returned to you in savings on utility bills

We are now ready to go into the finishing phase. The information given in the next series of steps will help you make the necessary decisions about the finishing of your house

NOTES:

Step # 16 Interior walls and Ceilings: Materials and finishes

After all the mechanical work and insulation is completed, it is now time to proceed with the interior finishing process. It is important for you to confirm with your builder that all mechanical work and insulation has been checked and inspected before the finishing begins. I recommend that you meet with your builder and go over the house again before you begin the process of finishing. You want to be sure that nothing has been missed before closing up the walls and ceilings, because it is very costly to make corrections after this process is completed.

The process of finishing the interior of your house should be carefully planned. It is wise to discuss your interior decorating plan with your builder. If your situation allows, an interior decorator can be very helpful. If you do not feel that you can spend the money for a decorator, you can find ideas in books and magazines.

The following is a list of items that are used for the wall and ceiling surfaces and finishes. You can use this list to help you to choose the materials and finish that is best suited for your house. You should consult with your builder about these materials and finishes to assist you in the decision making process.

1) Sheetrock with smooth finish: painted, wallpaper, or tile
2) Sheetrock with textured finish: pre-finished when applied or painted
3) Plaster or stucco: pre-finished when applied or painted
4) Paneling: pre-finished or stained
5) Plywood: painted or stained
6) Wood boards: pre-finished, painted or stained.

The items listed above deal with the interior walls and ceilings. In the steps that follow we will cover the other areas of the finishing process.

NOTES:

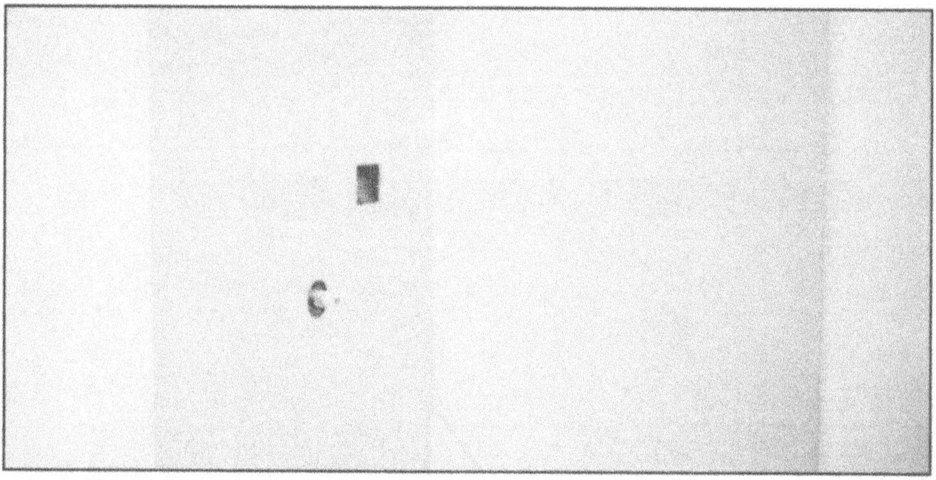

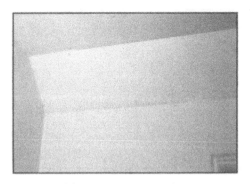 

Step # 17   Interior trimwork

The decorating scheme will dictate the type of interior trimwork that you choose for your house. Just as the paint colors, wallpaper, and other finishes play a role in your plan, so does the type of interior trim.

You should look through the same books and magazines that gave you ideas for the overall decorating scheme to help you choose the type of trimwork to use.

The following is a list of interior trimwork options to consider:

1) Interior doors
2) Door trim
3) Window trim
4) Base boards
5) Standard crown molding
6) Built-up crown molding
7) Accent trimwork
    Nitches
    Arches
    Beams
    Soffits
8) Chair railing
9) Wall panel molding
10) Stair parts:
    Treads
    Risers
    Posts
    Ballisters
    Railing
11) Fireplace mantles and trimwork.

There are other areas that are involved with the interior trimwork that really are not part of the decoration, but are functional parts of the house. These areas should also be discussed with your builder.

1) Closet shelving
2) Pantry and storage shelving
3) Cedar lined closets or storage areas
4) Attic accessibility and storage
5) Garage shelving, storage, and work benches.

These are a few things that will assist you in discussing the interior trimwork with your builder. It is very important to keep the line of communication open with your builder. You should tell your builder what you want to accomplish for the interior decoration. I will repeat this statement, your builder has been through this process before; therefore, you should allow your builder to help you with not only the functional parts of the interior but with the interior decorating.

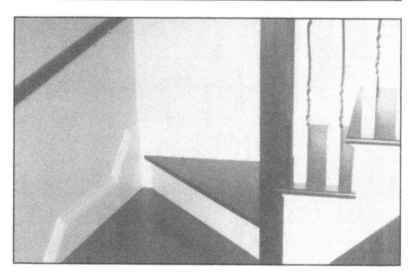

Step # 18   Cabinetry

The cabinetry that you choose will not only enhance the interior design of your house but also serves as a functional part of your house. The cabinetry can be custom built or factory built. Your builder will assist you in choosing the better of the two sources for your situation. The following is a list of items that you will need to discuss with your builder and the cabinetry person. These items need to be discussed whether custom or factory built cabinetry will be used for your house.

1) Quality of construction
2) Materials available
3) Styles available
4) Finishes available
5) Hardware available
6) Counter tops available
   Styles
   Colors
   Materials
7) Kitchen cabinetry
8) Appliance lay-out
9) Desk area cabinetry
10) Pantry cabinetry
11) Island cabinetry
12) Eating or serving bars
13) Wet bar
14) Laundry room cabinetry
15) Bathroom cabinetry
16) Dressing area cabinetry
17) Closet cabinetry and shelving
18) Built-in cabinetry in any areas
19) Raised-panel trimwork
20) Fireplace mantles and trimwork.

These areas should be discussed in detail with your builder and cabinetry person in order for you to get the cabinetry that you desire to add to your interior plan .

NOTES:

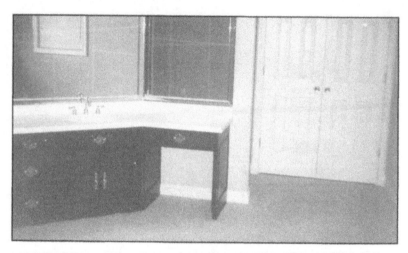

Step # 19 Hardware and accessories

Another part of the finishing process of your house is choosing your hardware and accessories. The following is a list of items to discuss with your builder concerning these areas:

1) Appliances:
   Stove or cooktop
   Conventional oven
   Microwave oven
   Dishwasher
   Trash compactor
   Refrigerator
   Washer and dryer
   Wet bar icemaker
   Wet bar refrigerator
2) Door knobs and locksets for the interior and exterior doors
3) Kick plates, and other door accessories
4) Bathroom accessories
5) Medicine cabinets
6) Mirrors
7) Shower doors and enclosures
8) Interior glass for cabinets
9) Gas logs for fireplaces.

NOTES:

Step # 20 Floor coverings

There are many types of floor coverings available. The overall interior design of your home will dictate the type of floor coverings used.

1) Hardwood
2) Parquet
3) Carpet
4) Sheet vinyl
5) Vinyl tile
6) Ceramic tile
7) Quarry tile
8) Marble
9) Granite
10) Slate
11) Stone

Each item of floor covering listed, varies in cost, style, color, and process of installation. It is important that you discuss with your builder, early in the project, the particular type of floor coverings that you plan to use. This will allow you to choose the floor coverings that are best suited to your budget and decorating plan. Your builder will also need to make the proper provisions and preparations for the installation of your chosen floor coverings.

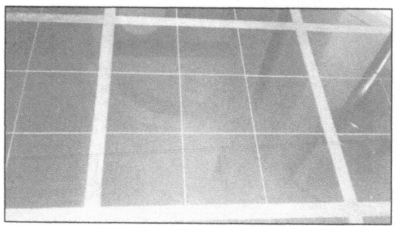

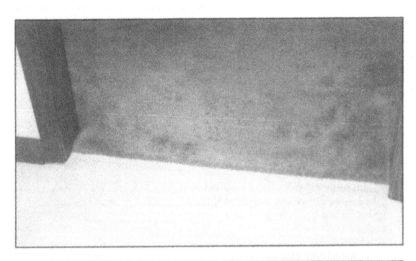

Step # 21 Exterior surfaces

The interior part of the house finishing and decorating should now be well on the way to completion. There are only two steps left to cover in our guide.

The following is a list of exterior options that you should discuss with your builder. You should remember that your builder will assist you in choosing the items that best meets your needs for cost, design, maintenance and durability:

1) Wood decks and railings:
   - Redwood
   - Cedar
   - Cypress
   - Treated pine
2) Porches and patios
   - Wood floor and railings:
   - Hard surface floors: regular concrete, aggregate concrete, brick, or stone
   - Masonry railings: Brick walls and columns or stone posts and railing
   - Ornamental iron railings
3) Fencing:
   - Wood
   - Brick walls and columns
   - Ornamental iron posts and railing
4) Walkways:
   - Regular concrete
   - Aggregate concrete
   - Stamped concrete
   - Brick
   - Stone
5) Driveways and Parking areas:
   - Regular concrete
   - Aggregate concrete
   - Stamped concrete
   - Asphalt
   - Gravel

The items listed are all part of the exterior finishing process for your house and they will be associated with our last point of discussion.

NOTES:

Step # 22 Landscaping

Landscaping, when done properly, enhances the beauty of any house. You should check with your builder about a landscape designer to assist you. After choosing your landscape designer, you should meet with that person and your builder to discuss the landscaping for your house and property. The following is a list of items that should be discussed and planned for this final, yet very important, step in completing your house.

1) Site drainage
2) Grading and earthwork
3) Seeding or sodding the yard
4) Planting area lay-outs
5) Pool or fountain installation
6) Sprinkler system
7) Landscape lighting
8) Driveway and parking area lay-outs and finish surfaces
9) Walkway lay-outs and finish surfaces
10) Fencing and walled-in areas

During the meeting with your landscape designer and builder, you should discuss plant types, budget, and overall design.. The landscape designer will then make arrangements to meet with you at a later date to present possible landscape plans. You should remember that the landscaping process can be completed over a period of time, depending upon your financial situation.

NOTES:

Conclusion:

In this step by step guide, I have tried to give you as much information as I could to assist you in building your house. The ideas that I have given you are simply those that I feel will help you enjoy this experience. I said earlier that building should be challenging, yet enjoyable, and I hope that you will use this guide to make building your house, a challenging, fulfilling, and enjoyable experience for all involved.

Thank you very much—

Note:

I hope that you will decide to use my Photo album and log to keep an accurate account of the process of building your house. These will be items that will be very special to you and your family in the future.

NOTES

Printed in the USA
CPSIA information can be obtained
at www.ICGtesting.com
JSHW082226140824
68134JS00015B/753